People Who Help Us

LEVEL 8
/ea/

Teaching Tips

Purple Level 8

This book focuses on the grapheme **/ea/**.

Before Reading
- Discuss the title. Ask readers what they think the book will be about. Have them support their answer.
- Discuss the book's focused grapheme: /ea/. Explain that it can have three different sounds: long /e/, short /e/, and long /a/. Give examples of each, such as *eat*, *bread*, and *break*.

Read the Book
- Encourage readers to read independently, either aloud or silently to themselves.
- Prompt readers to break down unfamiliar words into units of sound and string the sounds together to form the words. Then, ask them to look for context clues to see if they can figure out what these words mean. Discuss new vocabulary to confirm meaning.
- Urge readers to point out when the focused phonics grapheme appears in the text. What sound is it making?

After Reading
- Ask readers comprehension questions about the book. What helpers did you see in the book? What other community helpers do you know?
- Encourage readers to think of words with the /ea/ grapheme. On a separate sheet of paper, have them write the words. Group them by the different /ea/ sounds.

© 2024 Booklife Publishing
This edition is published by arrangement with Booklife Publishing.

North American adaptations © 2024 Jump!
5357 Penn Avenue South
Minneapolis, MN 55419
www.jumplibrary.com

Decodables by Jump! are published by Jump! Library.
All rights reserved. No part of this book may be reproduced in any form without written permission from the publisher.

Library of Congress Cataloging-in-Publication Data is available at www.loc.gov or upon request from the publisher.

ISBN: 979-8-88524-784-9 (hardcover)
ISBN: 979-8-88524-785-6 (paperback)
ISBN: 979-8-88524-786-3 (ebook)

Photo Credits

Images are courtesy of Shutterstock.com. Cover – 3 - Duplass, Regien Paassen, New Africa, Mega Pixel. p4–5 – Pixel-Shot, Rido. p6–7 - Kzenon, Peakstock. p8–9 – Drazen Zigic, VDB Photos. p10–11 – Prostock-studio, hedgehog94. p12–13 – bibiphoto, Lotusstudio. p14–15 – Monkey Business Images, Ormalternative. p16 – Shutterstock.

How many people can you think of who help you?

There are lots of people who help us. We can do lots of things without help, but there are lots of things that we need people to help us with.

Some people help us stay healthy. Some people grow the things we need to make food so that we can eat. There are teachers and vets too. The list goes on!

Lots of people help us stay healthy. They can help us if we break a bone or if we tear our skin. Ouch! These people can help us feel better in no time!

Health is not just about when we have a bump or a cut. It can be if we have problems that do not hurt. Some people help us if we are deaf or blind.

Mail is the letters and packages that get sent to us. There are lots of people that help mail get from place to place.

First, the address on the mail is read, and then the mail is sorted. Then a driver brings the mail where it is meant to go. They drop mail off for us in all sorts of weather!

Mail truck

When pets are not well, sometimes we cannot help them feel better. We can head to the vet to get help. Vets look after the health of animals.

Vets can help pets feel better. They can visit farms too. Vets help farmers keep the farm animals healthy.

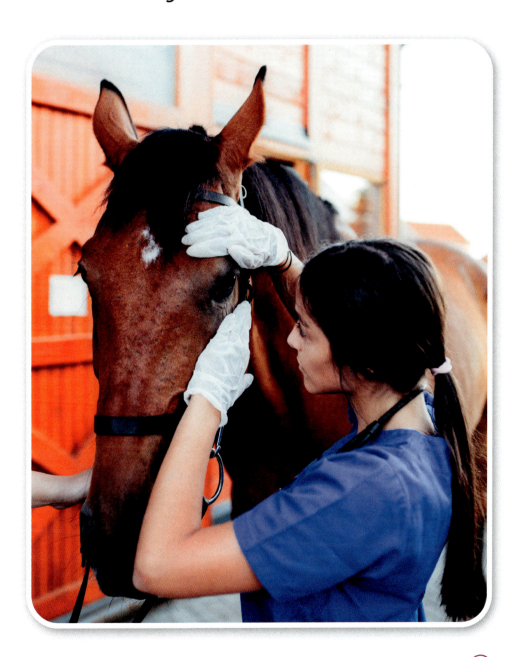

Farmers help us get the food we need. Farming is a job that goes on all year round. Farmers spread seeds all over the soil. The seeds then grow into crops.

Farmers grow hay in meadows.

Crops can then be sent to the store as they are, or they can be turned into something new. Wheat can be used to make things such as bread and pasta.

Teachers help us in school. You might have the same teacher for all subjects, or you might have a different teacher for each.

Some teachers might help you with math problems. Other teachers might help you read interesting books like this one. Some will even help you paint things to take home!

Say the name of each object below. Is the "ea" in each a short /e/ sound or a long /e/ sound?

beaver

read

breakfast

feather